What Is on Top?

A BOOK ABOUT POSITIONS

BY NICK REBMAN

Published by The Child's World®
1980 Lookout Drive • Mankato, MN 56003-1705
800-599-READ • www.childsworld.com

Acknowledgments
The Child's World®: Mary Swensen, Publishing Director
Red Line Editorial: Editorial direction and production
The Design Lab: Design

Photographs ©: Roberto A. Sanchez/iStockphoto, cover (top left); Donald Erickson/iStockphoto (bottom right); iStockphoto (top right), (bottom left), 4; Shutterstock Images, 5, 6-7, 12-13; Syda Productions/Shutterstock Images, 8; Carsten Reisinger/ Shutterstock Images, 9; monkeybusinessimages/iStockphoto, 10-11

ISBN 9781503807693
LCCN 2015958147

Printed in the United States of America
Mankato, MN
June, 2016
PA02306

About the Author

Nick Rebman likes to write, draw, and travel. He lives in Minnesota.

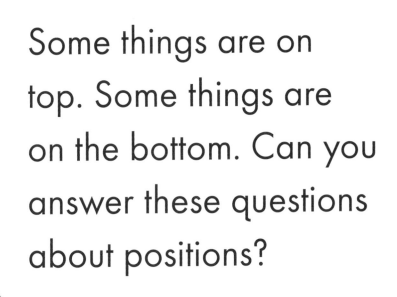

Some things are on top. Some things are on the bottom. Can you answer these questions about positions?

Brooke is making snacks. First she gets crackers. Then she puts cheese on them. Then she puts olives on them.

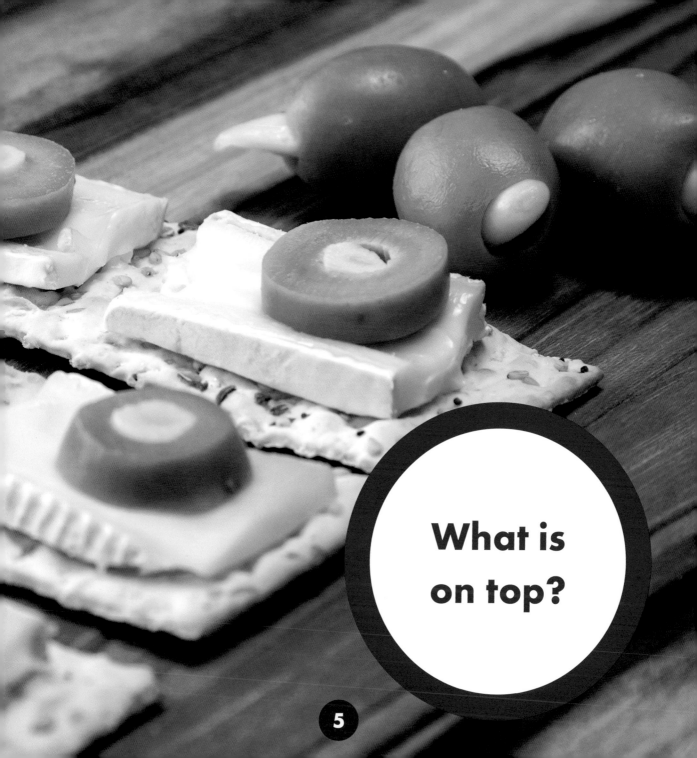

What is on top?

Riley is building a tower. First she puts down orange blocks. Then she adds green and blue blocks. Then she adds red blocks.

Which blocks are on the bottom?

Kayla and her parents are driving. They see a traffic light. The lights are red, yellow, and green.

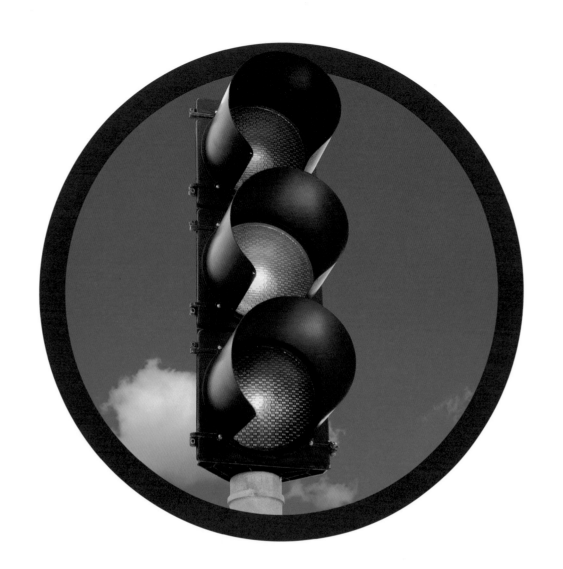

What light is in the middle?

The school day has started. The students sit at their table. The teacher stands by the whiteboard.

Who is in the front of the room?

11

The family is camping. Julia climbs on her dad's back. Oliver puts on his boots.

Who is
outside
the tent?

13

ANSWER KEY

The olives are on top.

The orange blocks
are on the bottom.

The yellow light is
in the middle.

The teacher is in the front.

Oliver is outside the tent.

GLOSSARY

bottom (BAH-tum) The bottom is the lowest. Riley's orange blocks were on the bottom.

front (FRUNT) The front is the forward part. The teacher stood in the front of the room.

middle (MI-dull) The middle is between two things. The yellow light was in the middle.

outside (owt-SIDE) Outside is the area around something. Oliver was outside the tent.

top (TOP) The top is the highest. Brooke's olives were on top.

TO LEARN MORE

IN THE LIBRARY

Pistoia, Sara. *Measurement*. Mankato, MN: Child's World, 2014.

Pistoia, Sara. *Patterns*. Mankato, MN: Child's World, 2014.

ON THE WEB

Visit our Web site for links about positions: **childsworld.com/links**

Note to Parents, Teachers, and Librarians: We routinely verify our Web links to make sure they are safe and active sites. So encourage your readers to check them out!

INDEX

blocks, 6

camping, 12

colors, 6, 8

school, 10

snacks, 4

students, 10

teachers, 10

traffic lights, 8